The Comp Guitar Player

by Russ Shipton

Book 3

Useful Information

Strumming Style

Bass-Strum Style

Arpeggio Style

Alternating Thumb Style

Classical Style

Lyrics

Songs & Music

Wise Publications London / New York / Paris / Sydney / Copenhagen / Madrid / Tokyo

Scales

Did you try that bit of homework I gave you at the end of Book 2? Well, if you found it difficult, you'll find the answers to my questions on this page. In a sense, most western music is bound up with the idea of the major scale, so the 'Do Re Mi Fa So La Ti Do' that you've known for some time is more important than you may have thought!

What Is A Scale?

A scale is a series of notes that starts and ends with a note of the same name (but an octave higher). There are various scales, but the major scale, with 8 notes and intervals of: tone, tone, semitone, tone, tone, tone, semitone, is the one which is most important...

The **C** Major Scale

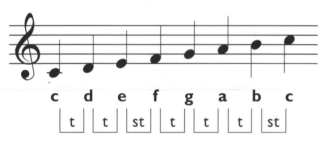

Intervals... **t** = tone   **st** = semi-tone

The Scale And The Melody

You may be wondering what the connection is between the major scale and the songs and accompaniments that you've been singing and playing.

Well, when playing in the key of **C** for example (that usually means starting and ending with a **C** chord), it means that all the melody notes and probably the accompanying notes as well, will normally be from the major scale of the key note, in this case the **C** major scale.

The Scale And Bass Runs

You may have noticed that the common bass runs used in Book 2 are part of the scale. The last half of the scale of **C** is the run you used from the **G** chord to the **C** chord; **g**, **a**, **b**, and **c** to finish.

Other Major Scales

Because some chords are a lot easier to finger than others, most guitarists (particularly modern players) will play in the keys of **C**, **G**, **D**, **A**, and **E** (or they might use a capo). The key of **C**, as you see above, has no sharp or flat notes. The others involve one or more notes being sharpened, so that the same intervals exist between the notes. Let's have a look at the **G** major scale...

The **G** Major Scale★ (**f** is sharp)

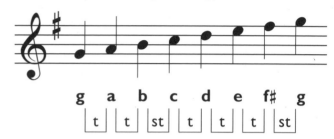

If you look at the gaps or intervals between the notes, you'll notice that only the **f** note must be altered. By making it an **f♯**, it is now a whole tone from the **e** note, and a semi-tone to the **g** note.

Now try the **D** Major Scale★ (**f** and **c** are sharp)

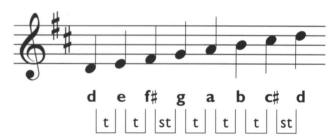

As with the **G** scale, we have to check the gaps between the notes. For a major scale, they should always be: tone, tone, semi-tone, tone, tone, tone, semi-tone. So the **f** and **c** notes must both be sharpened. Now see if you can work out the notes in the **A** and **E** major scales. All you have to do is to keep the same intervals that the major scale must always have, and flatten or sharpen any notes where necessary.

On the next page we'll look at the relationship of the major scale and chords, but before moving on, practise playing these five scales at the lower end of the fingerboard, and try to remember the notes as you play them.

★ *The sharp signs (♯), at the beginning of a stave, tell you that all those notes, high or low, are always played sharp.*

Chords

Now you've got the idea of the major scale, on this page we'll see how the chords you've been using are related to it.

What's A Chord?

A chord is produced when three notes or more are played or held at the same time. These notes are normally found in the major scale of the key that the melody is in, and are either the same as the melody note, or harmonise with it. The chords that you've learnt so far have notes that are always certain intervals apart - intervals that are most natural or pleasing to the ear.

Where Do Chords Come From?

In any particular key, the chords you'd expect to find in an accompaniment come from the major scale of the key or 'tonic' note. Three very important chords are those with their root notes (the note that gives the chord its name) in the 1st, 4th and 5th positions of the scale...

The **C** Major Scale

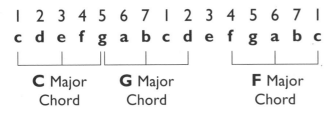

A common major chord consists of three notes: the root note, plus the note two steps above it, plus the note two steps above that one. So the **C** chord (**C** Major chord, in full) has the **c**, **e** and **g** notes in it, while the **F** and **G** chords have **f**, **a** and **c**, and **g**, **b** and **d** notes respectively. One important alternative to the **G** chord is the **G7** chord. This has 4 notes in it: the **g**, **b** and **d** of the **G** chord plus the **f** note.

Apart from the three most important chords shown for the **C** Major Scale, what other chords might you expect in an accompaniment? Well, any of the chords that have their root notes in the other positions of the scale. So, returning to the scale, let's see what chords emerge, if we take two other notes and the root note in the same way as above...

The **C** Major Scale

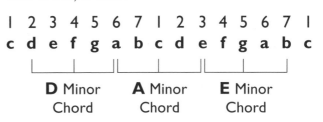

So there are three major chords, **C**, **F** and **G**, plus three minor chords **Dm**, **Em** and **Am**. One more chord, the **B** diminished, would be produced from the **b** (the root note) + the **d** + the **f**, but this diminished chord isn't used as much as the others.

Other Keys

Just as the major scale intervals stay the same, so do the type of chords. Let's have a look at the **G** major scale, and what chords to expect when a song is in the key of **G**...

The **G** Major Scale

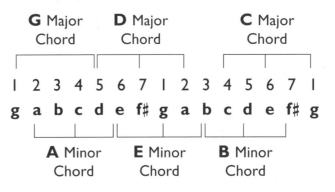

See if you can do the same thing for the keys of **D**, **A**, and **E**.

Chord Variations

So far you've seen slight variations to the usual 3-note major and minor chords. The 7th and minor 7th chords include one more note. You've also played a **sus4** (suspended 4th) chord. Look above and you'll see that the 4th note of the **C** scale is **f**, so to produce a **Csus4** chord, the **f** note is added to the normal **C** major chord, while the **e** note (the 3rd) is taken away.

Chord variations are used more in popular music today, and some are used in the accompaniments for the two Oasis songs in the first section.

Jamaica Farewell

Traditional, arranged by Russ Shipton

↓T	= Thumb strum down
↓	= Strum down
↑	= Strum up

More Syncopation

You're off to the Caribbean for the first song of the book! The calypso pattern involves more syncopation, i.e. stress on the offbeat. In fact there are two downstrums on the offbeat and an upstrum on the beat, and the thumb is used to glide across the strings after beat 1. If you prefer to use a flatpick, make the offbeat downstrums shorter than usual.

Accompaniment: 4/4 Rhythm

Melody

The first line uses these notes:

d d d d e f♯ g
Down the way where the nights are gay

f♯ e d d c c c b c d
And the sun shines daily on the mountain top.

Notice that all the notes above are from the **G** major scale (shown on page 3), as are the rest of the notes in the song.

Strumming Style

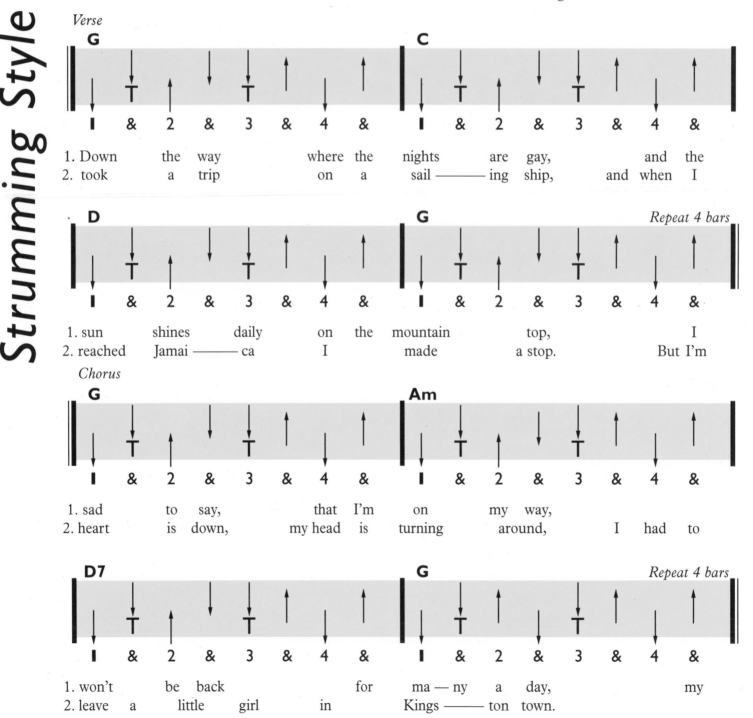

Wonderwall

Noel Gallagher

Altered Chords

Guitarists today often use altered chords, where the fingering is unusual or a note (or two) is added to the standard shape. The accompaniment for 'Wonderwall' involves many chords of this kind, three of which have exactly the same name!

Cmaj7 Chord

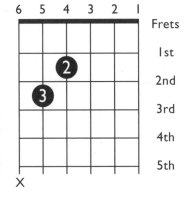

Em7 Chord

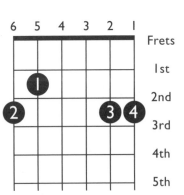

A7sus4(2) **Chord**

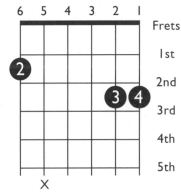

G Chord

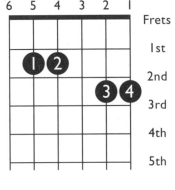
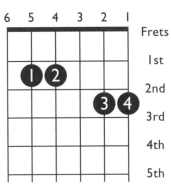

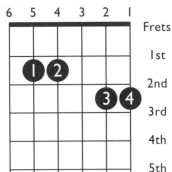

G/F# Chord

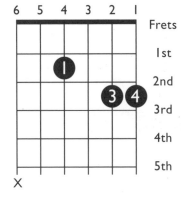

Dsus4 Chord

A7sus4(3) **Chord**

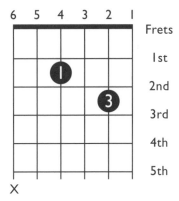

A7sus4(1) **Chord**

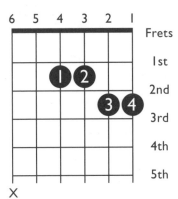
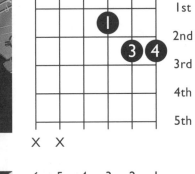

Cadd9 Chord

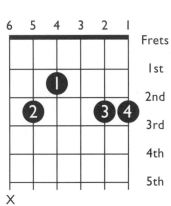

Strumming Style

5

Wonderwall

Oasis

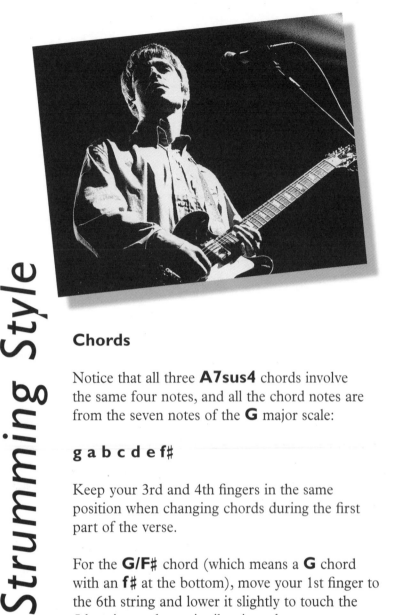

Strumming Style

Chords

Notice that all three **A7sus4** chords involve the same four notes, and all the chord notes are from the seven notes of the **G** major scale:

g a b c d e f♯

Keep your 3rd and 4th fingers in the same position when changing chords during the first part of the verse.

For the **G/F♯** chord (which means a **G** chord with an **f♯** at the bottom), move your 1st finger to the 6th string and lower it slightly to touch the 5th string and stop it vibrating when you strum across the chord.

Rhythm Variations

The main rhythmic feel for this accompaniment is semiquavers, with *downstrums between beats*. As before, make the downstrums on the beats longer and heavier. Some bars have syncopation, with a stress on the semiquaver upstrum before and after beat 3. Make these upstrums longer than usual and do downward airstrokes on beat 3 and halfway between beats 3 and 4.

Sometimes the syncopated stress is only on the upstrum before beat 3, as in the third bar shown (starting with **C maj7**).

General

The speed of this and the next song should be about 90 beats or crotchets per minute, or in standard notation 'andante', which means reasonably slow. If you want to play along with the original recording put your capo on the 2nd fret and play the chord shapes given.

Melody

The first line is shown below. Like the chords in the accompaniment, all the melody notes are from the **G** major scale.

b a g a g a g a a   g   a g
Today is gonna be the day that they're gonna

a   g   a b g
throw it back to you.

Accompaniment: 4/4 Rhythm

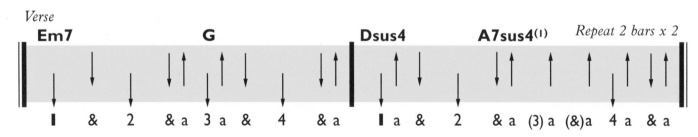

1.   To — day   is gonna be the day that they're gonna throw it back to you.
2.   By   now   you should have some-how re-a – lised what you got - ta do.
3. I don't be – lieve that   any   body   feels   the way I   do   a – bout you

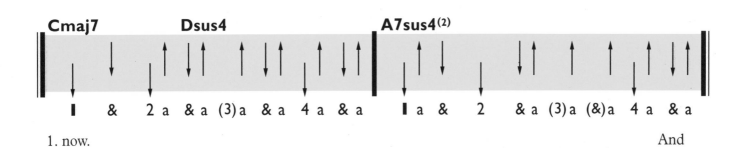

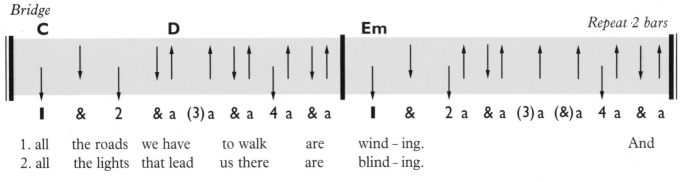

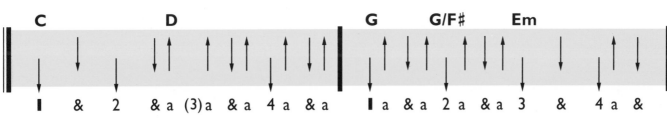

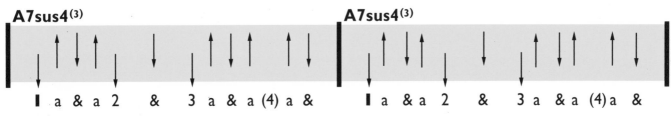

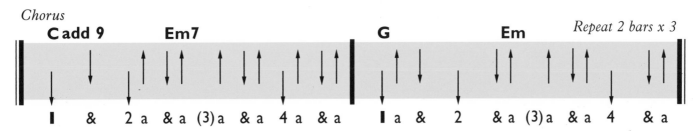

Strumming Style

Don't Look Back In Anger

Oasis

Strumming Style

Chords

Two new chords occur in this arrangement:

Fm6 Chord

A♭dim Chord (A♭ diminished)

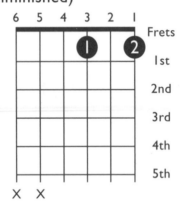

The **Fm6** is similar to the **F** chord but with the 3rd and 4th fingers removed. Both chords include one note that is out of key, i.e. not from the **C** major scale.

Rhythm Patterns

Like the last song, this accompaniment involves semiquavers and downstrums between beats. It should also be played reasonably slowly. There is no syncopation this time, but many slight pattern changes to look out for.

Melody

e d d c d c e dca

Slip inside the eye of your mind

All the melody notes are in key, except the **e♭** for 'take' in the bridge section. The occasional use of out-of-key notes and chords creates a little tension and more interest.

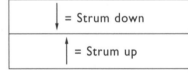

↓ = Strum down

↑ = Strum up

Accompaniment: 4/4 Rhythm

Verse

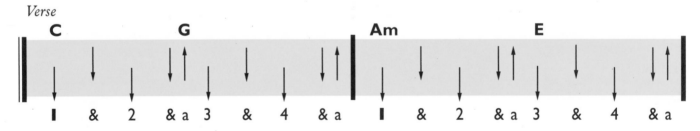

C   G   Am   E

1 & 2 & a 3 & 4 & a   1 & 2 & a 3 & 4 & a

1. Slip in-side   the eye   of   your   mind,   don't you know you might find
2. You   said   that you'd   nev — er   been,   but all the things that you've seen

Repeat 4 bars

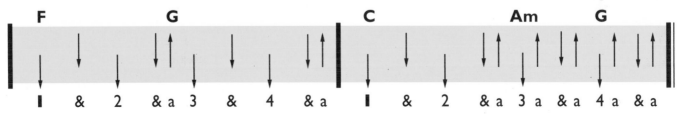

F   G   C   Am   G

1 & 2 & a 3 & 4 & a   1 & 2 & a 3 a & a 4 a & a

1.   a better place to play.
2.   slowly   fade   a-way.

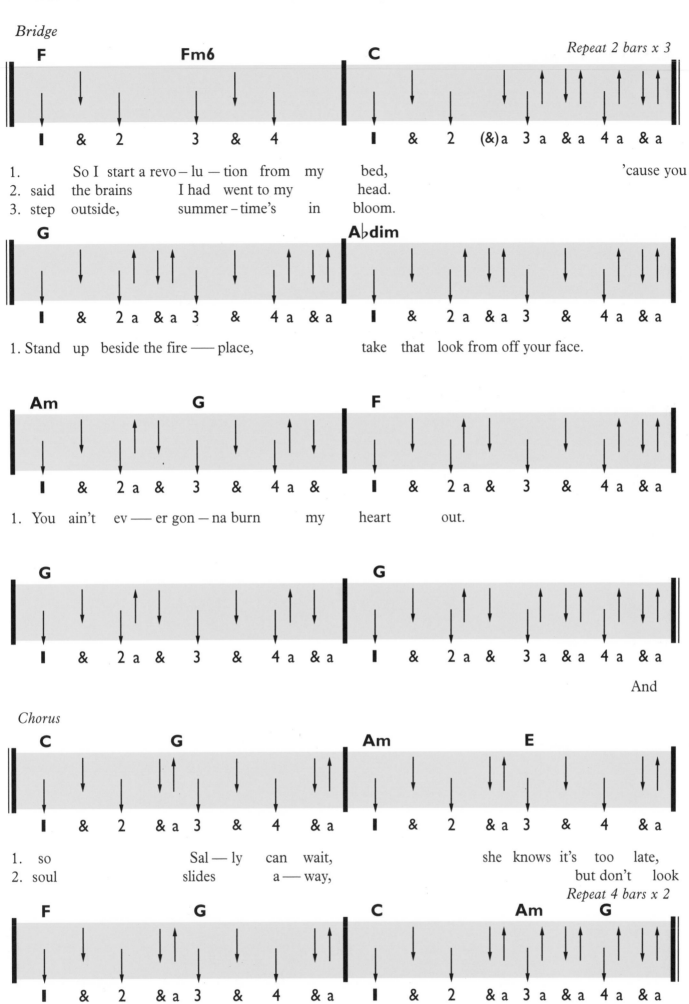

Lay Down Sally

Eric Clapton

Strumming Style

Boogies

The boogie is a special type of rhythmic accompaniment which normally involves adding a '6th' note to the chord on the 2nd and 4th beats. This note is called a 6th because it is six steps above the chord root note (see page 3). The strums are much shorter than usual and the chord shapes are not standard. This is the simplest way that the **A**, **D** and **E** chords can be held for playing 'Lay Down Sally':

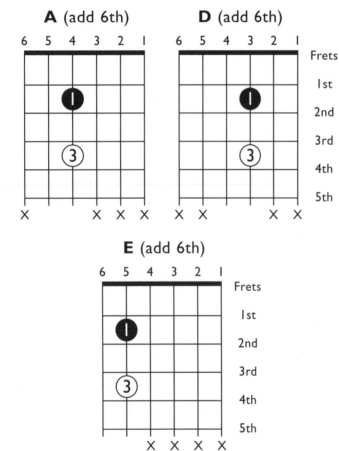

Accompaniment: 4/4 Rhythm

Rhythm Patterns

Just two strings are played for each chord, so both downstrums and upstrums are short. Add the 6th note on the 2nd beat of each bar and then remove it immediately. Add the 6th again on the 4th beat. Remove it again before you play the 1st beat of the next bar.

Two alternating patterns are given, and both involve the 6th note being added on the 2nd and 4th beats. Keep the flatpick (or fingers) near the strings and only move the right hand a little.

Damping

A very important technique for playing 'heavier' guitar accompaniments involves stopping strings from ringing on after clear notes have been sounded. This can be done by the left hand fingers releasing the pressure on the strings but still keeping contact with them.

When you've mastered the boogie patterns given for 'Lay Down Sally', try damping the 6th note that is added on the 2nd and 4th beats. Add the 3rd finger, do the strum and then release the pressure but keep touching the string. Make the note last just short of half a beat.

Melody

This song has a blues feel to it, which explains the use of the natural **g** note in the scale of **A** major. Here's the first line of lyrics with notes:

g g g a b b a
There is nothing that is wrong

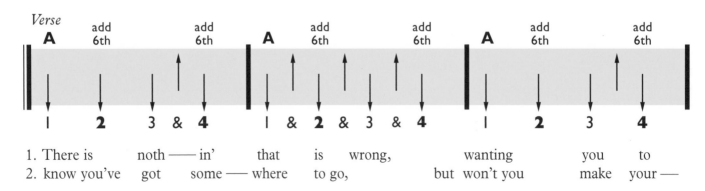

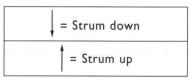

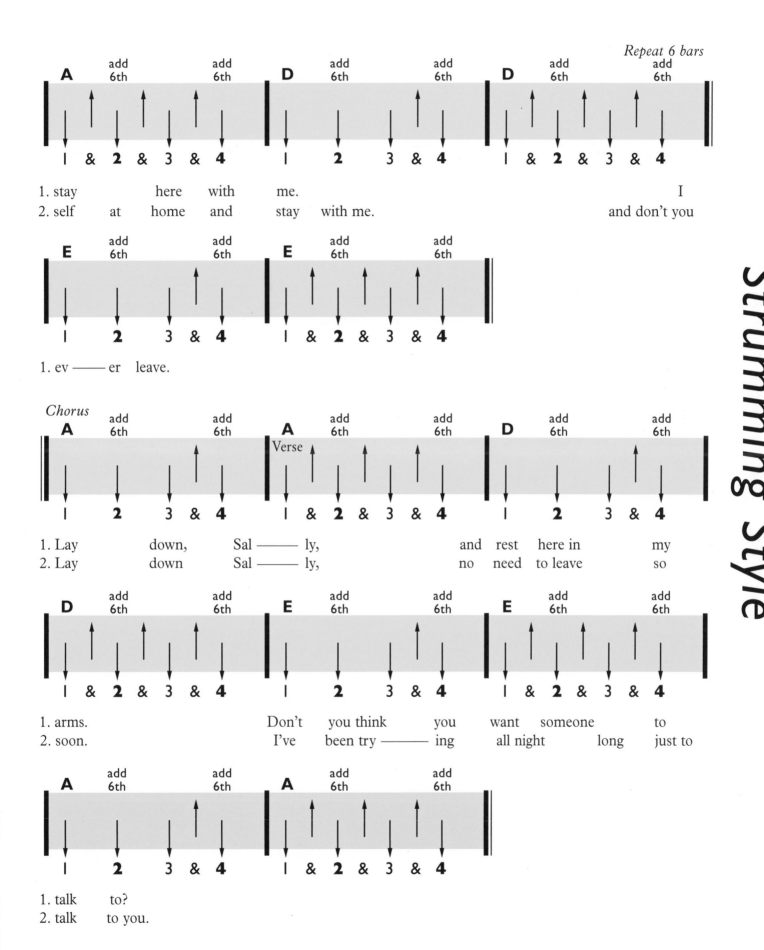

Words & Music by Eric Clapton, Marcy Levy & George Terry
© Copyright 1977 & 1999 Eric Clapton (33.33%) & Throat Music/
Warner Chappell Music Limited, Griffin House, 161 Hammersmith Road, London W6 (66.67%).
All Rights Reserved. International Copyright Secured.

Can't Buy Me Love

The Beatles

WarmUp

Bass-Strum Style

Swing Bass-Strum

You've already used the swing rhythm in the strumming style. Some bass-strum songs also need to be swung, and as before, the upstrums between beats are delayed (as indicated visually) to produce a jumpy feel.

New Chord Shapes

'Can't Buy Me Love' has a blues feel, and that means **7**th chords can be used instead of the normal major chords:

G7 Chord

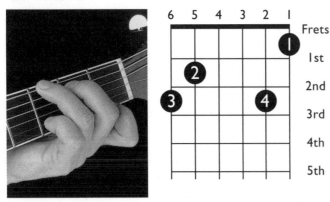

C7 Chord

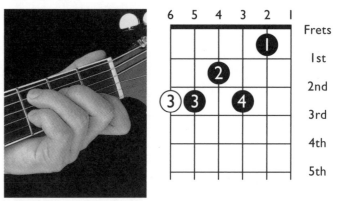

D7 Chord

This **G7** version includes the **d** note on the 2nd string held by the 4th finger. The **C7** shape is moved up two frets to produce this **D7** version.

If you strum across the open 1st string, that will create a **D9** chord. This 9th chord has five notes, including the 7th and 9th notes, **c** and **e**. The 3rd finger can be moved to the 6th string for the **C7** and **D7** chords, as shown.

Rhythm Pattern

One pattern is shown throughout but try making some changes to the number of upstrums and which bass string is struck. Repeat the twelve verse bars for Verse 2 before going to the chorus. Stop playing on the 1st beat of the last bar, sing 'Can't buy me' and then start the **Bm** bar.

For the **Bm** chord in this arrangement, you need to do a 'full' barre across all 6 strings.

$\frac{6}{T}$ = Thumb plays 6th string
↓ = Strum down
↑ = Strum up

Accompaniment: 4/4 Swing Rhythm

Verse

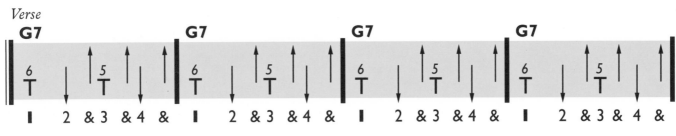

1. (I'll) Buy you a dia - mond ring my friend, if it makes you feel all right. I'll
2. (I'll) Give you all I've got to give if you say you'll love me too. I

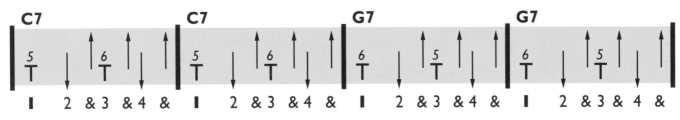

1. get you an — y ——— thing my friend, if it makes you feel all right. 'Cause
2. may not have a lot to give but what I've got I'll give to you.

Repeat 12 bars

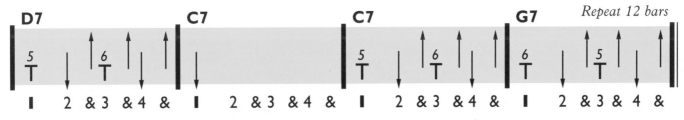

1. I don't care too much for money, money can't buy me love.
2. I don't care too much for money, money can't buy me love. 2. Can't buy me

Chorus

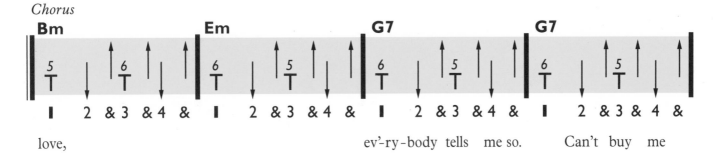

love, ev'-ry-body tells me so. Can't buy me

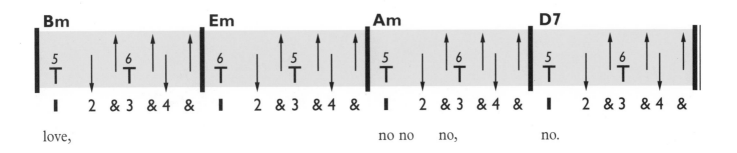

love, no no no, no.

Words & Music by John Lennon & Paul McCartney
© *Copyright 1964 Northern Songs.*
All Rights Reserved. International Copyright Secured.

She'll Be Coming Round The Mountain

Traditional, arranged by Russ Shipton

Two Parts

Now I have something special for you to try:
to learn two parts with different chord shapes and play one along with the other. The first part is the accompaniment in the key of **A** major with the **A**, **D** & **E** chords. For the second part, where the melody is picked out, *a capo is placed at the second fret* and the **G**, **C** & **D7** shapes are played.

Playing The Parts Together

Those of you working in the classroom can divide into two groups, and those at home can play along with a friend or a tape recorder.

First learn this simple accompaniment for a well-known traditional American song, which includes hammer-ons and runs...

Bass-Strum Style

Accompaniment: 4/4 Rhythm

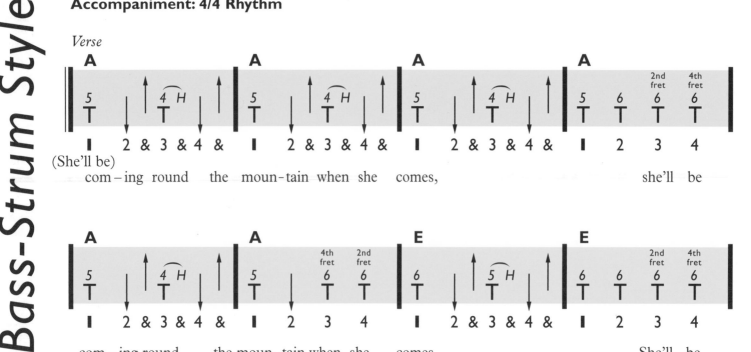

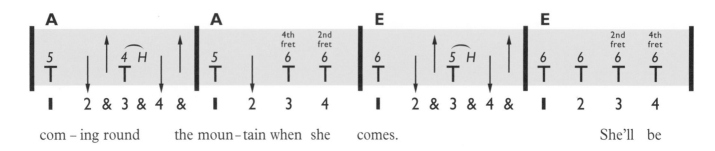

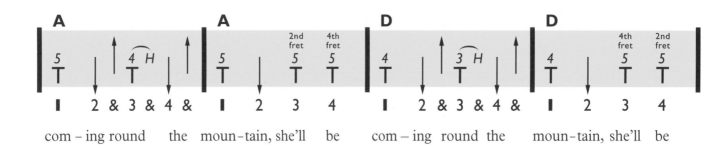

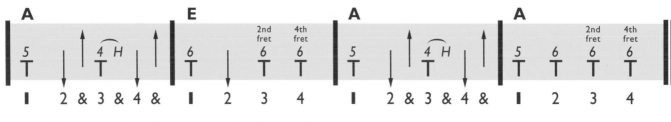

$\frac{5}{T}$ = Thumb plays 5th string
↓ = Strum down
↑ = Strum up

Picking Out The Melody

Go through this arrangement carefully. Hold the usual chords, but move the most convenient finger to play the melody notes that aren't in the shape you're holding. These are indicated by string and fret numbers. Picking out the tune means striking treble strings more than usual. The strums should be kept short.

In bar 3, hammer the 1st finger onto the 2nd fret 3rd string for the **a** note. In bar 6 the 3rd finger is moved to the 2nd string 3rd fret for the **d** note,

and can be left there for the following down/up strums. The top string is left open. Finally the 3rd finger is removed for an open 2nd string **b** note.

In the 8th and 12th bars, use your 4th finger for the **d** and **g** notes respectively. The **D7** bar near the end involves a bass run to **G**. Bring your 1st finger up for the **f♯**. Use your 1st finger for the two hammer-ons in the penultimate bar.

Solo: Capo 2nd fret G = A D7 = E7 C = D

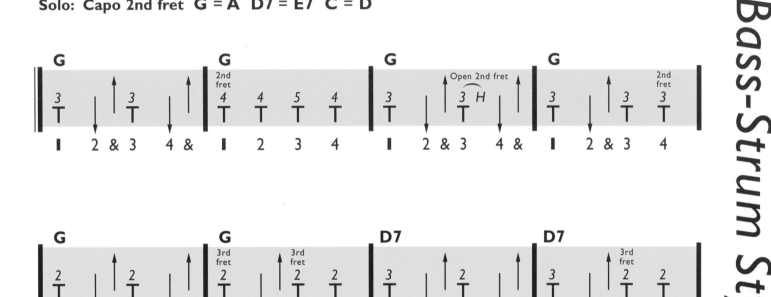

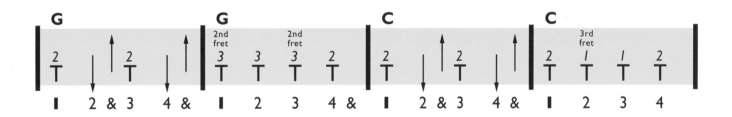

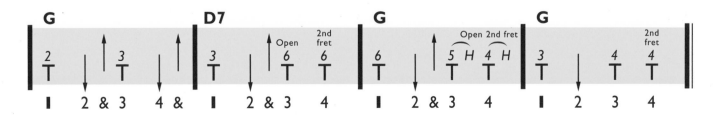

Suzanne

Leonard Cohen

Arpeggio Style

Syncopated Arpeggio

The pattern for this great Leonard Cohen song includes one thumb strike between beats. This offbeat stress suits ballads like 'Suzanne'. The middle strings are used to match the atmosphere of this haunting and intense song.

Watch for varied bass notes and quick hammer-ons. Move the 2nd finger to the 5th string for the **b** note of the slow bass run from **C** to **G** in bar 16.

Pinches

A two string pinch, where bass and treble strings are played at the same time, is also used in the arpeggio style. Use your thumb and 3rd finger (for the top string) at the start of five chorus bars.

D7/F♯ Chord

The **D7/F♯** chord (**D7** with **f♯** as bass) is another slightly altered chord that many guitarists use, especially in the key of **G** major. Hold the usual **D7** shape and bring the thumb over for the **F♯** on the 2nd fret of the 6th string.

Melody

The melody notes as well as chords are all in key except for an occasional **f** natural. Here is the first line of the melody:

d   d   d   d   e d d   d   d d   e d
Suzanne takes you down to her place by the river

Accompaniment: 4/4 Rhythm

Verse

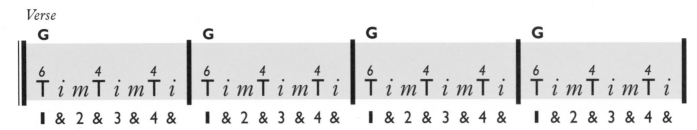

1. (Su-)zanne   takes   you   down,   to her place   near   the river,   you can
2. when you mean   to   tell her,   that you have   no love   to   give her,   then she

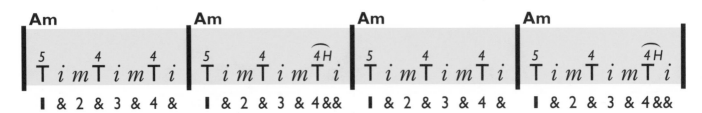

1. hear   the boats   go   by,   you can spend   the night   be — side   her,   and you
2. gets you   on   her wavelength,   and she   lets   the river   answer,   that you've

16

P	= Pinch thumb & Ring finger
T	= Thumb
i	= Index finger
m	= Middle finger
r	= Ring finger

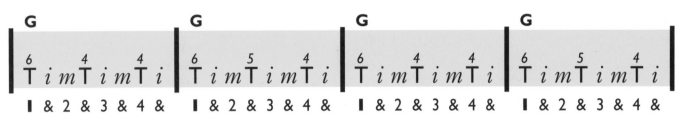

G   **G**   **G**   **G**

1. know that she's half crazy,   but that's why you want   to   be there,   and she
2. always been her lover.   And you
(to Chorus)

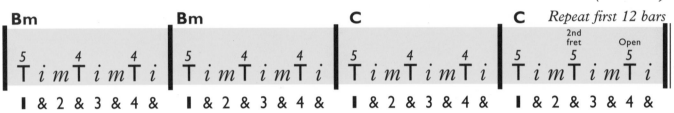

Bm   **Bm**   **C**   **C**   *Repeat first 12 bars*

1. feeds you tea and oranges   that come all the way   from China.   And just
(to start)

Chorus

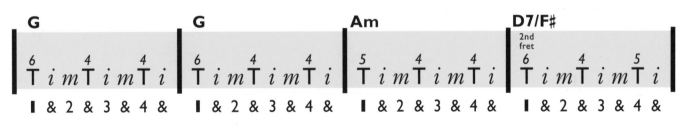

Bm   **Bm**   **C**   **C**

1. want to travel with her,   and you want to travel blind,   and you

G   **G**   **Am**   **D7/F#**

1. know that she will trust you, for you've touched her perfect body   with your

G   **G**

1. mind.

Words & Music by Leonard Cohen
© Copyright 1966 Project Seven Music, USA.
TRO-Essex Music Limited, Suite 2.07, Plaza 535 Kings Road, London SW10 for
the British Commonwealth (excluding Canada) and the Republic of Eire.
All Rights Reserved. International Copyright Secured.

Going Places

Russ Shipton

Arpeggio Style

Swing Arpeggio

The rhythm can be swung in all styles, and here's a swing arpeggio instrumental. Delay the notes between beats until just before the following beat. (The sign before the notation indicates that the beat note should be twice as long as the second note between beats).

This and the next piece are in standard notation to give you more practice at reading notes. Hold the chords indicated and you'll find the notes quickly.

Out-Of-Key Notes

This piece has a blues feel, so the **g** natural (not in the key scale of **E** major) sounds fine. It also makes changing chords easier! In bar 3 take your hand off the **E** chord and use your 1st finger for the **a♯**, which runs to **b**. Use your 3rd finger for the low **g** natural note in bars 5 and 6, again with your hand off the chord.

In bar 8 move your 2nd finger from the 5th to 6th string. Bars 9 and 10 involve more flattened, bluesy notes and the out-of-key chords **E7** and **Am**. You could use your 2nd, 3rd and 4th fingers for the **A** to make the change to **Am** easier.

Use the 1st finger for the **g** natural to **g♯** hammer-on in the last bar.

Accompaniment: 4/4 Swing Rhythm

Off The Wall

Russ Shipton

The Pull-Off

Another common embellishment is the 'pull-off', which in a sense is the opposite of the hammer-on. A fretted note is sounded by the right hand playing a string, then a second note is produced by the left hand finger coming off the string to an open string or a lower fret note.

The word 'pull' is used because the finger must pull or bend the string slightly (towards the ground) before lifting off. This ensures the second note will be loud enough.

Hold the 2nd fret of the 1st string with your 1st or 2nd finger. Sound the **f♯** note then pull the string slightly towards the ground and release the string to produce an open **e**.

General

Here's another opportunity for you to play in the 6/8 rhythm. Remember that the main stresses are on the 1st and 4th beats. This is made easier to read in standard notation because the two sets of three quavers are joined together.

Use the thumb for the bass strings and three fingers for the trebles, as usual.

Use the normal chord shapes and fingering. In the **D** chord bars the 2nd fret is pulled off to the open 1st string. Put the 2nd finger back when you need to play the **f♯**. In the **A** bars the 3rd finger is pulled off from the 2nd fret to the open 2nd string. The **E** bars mean pulling the 4th finger off from the 3rd fret to the open 2nd string.

Arpeggio Style

Accompaniment: 6/8 Rhythm

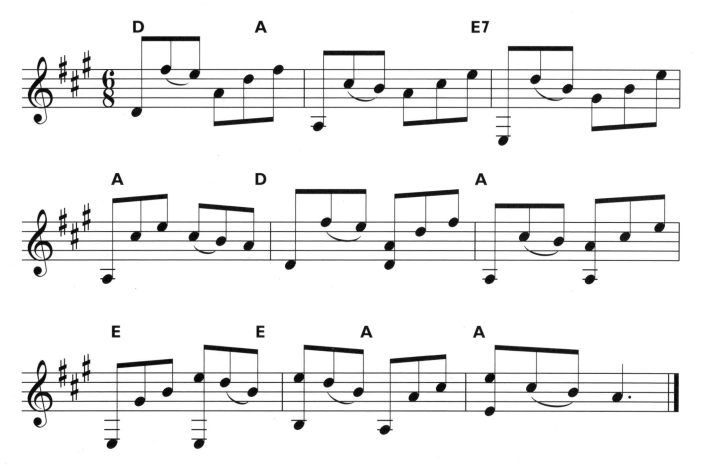

Always On My Mind

Willie Nelson

Arpeggio Style

This imitates the Willie Nelson recording, and is a short run to the **C** chord. For this pinch only, strike the 2nd string with your middle finger.

The last bar involves two quick chord changes on beats 3 and 4. This produces a strong and interesting 'push' back to the start of the next verse.

Chords

All the chords are fingered as usual for this accompaniment, apart from **Dm/C**. This requires a different fingering for the **Dm** chord. The 4th finger is placed on the 2nd string so the 3rd finger can hold the **c** note:

Dm/C Chord

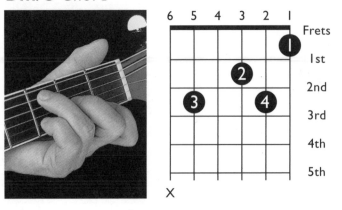

More Pattern Variations

The arrangement for this well-known ballad, made famous by both Willie Nelson and Elvis Presley, includes different kinds of syncopation, pinches, hammer-ons and a variety of bass runs. Go over each bar carefully.

Bar 1 of the lead-in has an offbeat thumb strike between beats 1 and 2. Bars 2 and 6 of the verse also include this syncopation. Notice the quick chord change on the last beat in bar 4 of the verse.

Melody

All the melody notes are in key, though the **D** chord is used for variety. Here is the first line:

e f gfe e d c ded dc b a
Maybe I didn't treat you quite as good as I should have

Accompaniment: 4/4 Rhythm

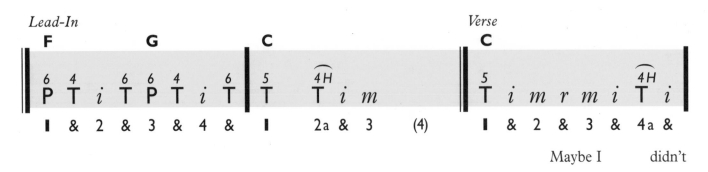

P	=	Pinch thumb & Ring finger
T	=	Thumb
i	=	Index finger
m	=	Middle finger
r	=	Ring finger

G

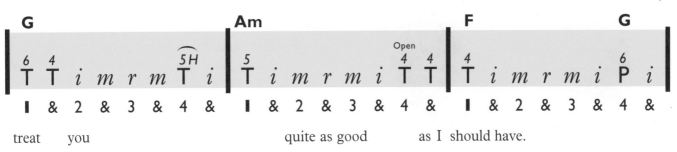

treat   you   quite as good   as I should have.

Maybe I   didn't love   you   quite as often   as I

could have.   If I made you feel   second best,

girl, I'm sorry   I was   blind.   You were al-ways on my

mind,   you were al-ways on my mind.

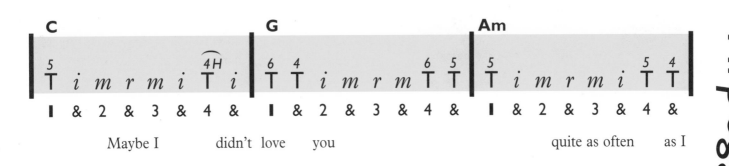

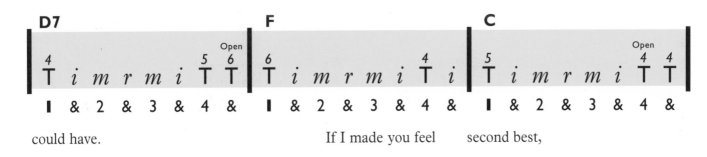

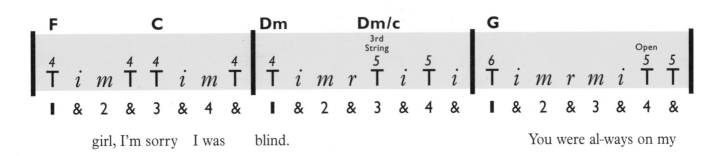

Arpeggio Style

Words & Music by Wayne Thompson, Mark James & Johnny Christopher

© Copyright 1971 (renewed 1979) Screen Gems-EMI Music Incorporated & Rose Bridge Music Incorporated, USA.
Screen Gems-EMI Music Limited, 127 Charing Cross Road, London WC2 (75%) & Chelsea Music Publishing Company Limited, 124 Great Portland Street, London W1 (25%).
All Rights Reserved. International Copyright Secured.

Imagine

John Lennon

Arpeggio Style

Slow Arpeggio

The arpeggio patterns you've played so far have been mid-tempo to fast. For some slower patterns, each beat is stressed more and plucks of more than one string can be used to fill out the sound:

4/4 Rhythm Finger **G**

		r		r		r	
⁶T	i	m	i	m	i	m	i
1	&	2	&	3	&	4	&

For the 3/4 rhythm remove the notes in the last beat. My arrangement of 'Imagine' includes ideas from the original, but to imitate John Lennon's piano style you could experiment with this kind of pattern. The chord comes on the beat with a pluck of three fingers, with the bass notes struck by the thumb between beats:

Accompaniment: 4/4 Rhythm

4/4 Rhythm Finger **C**

r			r			r			r		
m		5	m		5	m		5	m		5
i	T		i	T		i	T		i	T	
1	&	2	&	3	&	4	&				

Pattern Variations

The lead-in includes ideas from the original recording. Move your 3rd finger for the **f#** on the 4th fret of the 4th string. This is followed by the 2nd fret of the 4th string to begin the **C** bar, instead of the root note.

The end of this bar has a fast **e f f#** run on the 4th string. Use your 2nd, 3rd and 4th fingers. You could try a hammer-on from the **e** to **f**.

The 3rd bar then begins with the open **d** instead of the root note. A slow, downward bass run comes at the end of the verse, beginning with **c** and ending on **f#**. Raise your 2nd finger to the 5th string for the **b** and bring your 4th finger over for the **Am/G** chord. Use your thumb for the 6th string **f#** note of **D/F#**.

The middle section adds another bass note to the pattern occasionally. Use your 1st finger for the **a#** leading to **B7**. The final bar imitates the original recording with a run on the 6th string from **e** to **f** to **f#**. The **g** at the start of the next verse completes the run.

Melody

All the melody notes are in key, though the **B7** chord is used as a passing chord to add interest to the middle section. Here's the first line:

d d d   d   f# f# e   d   d d d f# f#e
Imagine there's no heaven, it's easy if you try

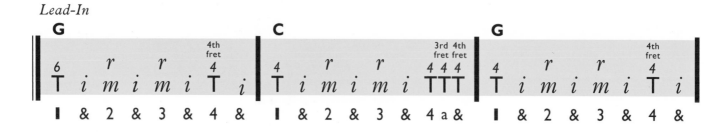

evidence

(Currie)

Capo 5th fret

```
        D         G              A    G
Saturday night the lights are all lit up
        D                        G        A
There's a bottle of wine beside an overfilled paper cup
        D              G           A    G
And the cigarette she left lit is all burned up
        D           G     A
But the heat from where she lay is not


                  G       D    A
Like smoke from factories   we leave out heat behind
                  G       D       A
Like wound down batteries  hearts stop sometimes
```

(same as verse 1)
And between these sheets her perfum lingers on
And in a couple of weeks
All the evidence will be gone

Like a dust free patch where a magazine lay
A girl leaves a gap when she goes
But a someone else fill sit up someday

(same as above)
Like smoke from factories
We leave out heat behind
Like wound down batteries
Hearts stop sometimes

```
A
  She took away the day dream
            D             G
Leaving nothing but daily life
Em               A       Asus4
  She took away almost everything
      D             A      G
But if you look you'll find evidence she left behind
```

(same as verse 1)
A blue bar of soap left on the sink
And lipstick round the last glass she used to drink
Those bruned up box of matches
That she kept
And heat in the matress where she slept

like smoke from factories
we leave out heat behind
like wound down batteries
hearts stop sometimes

like smoke from factories
we leave out heat behind
like wound down batteries
hearts stop sometimes

(repeat till fade)

*Lords of war
Revolver*

*12486
885 855*

|Chords| |Lyrics| |Submit| |Links| |Home| |News|

T	= Thumb
i	= Index finger
m	= Middle finger
r	= Ring finger

Arpeggio Style

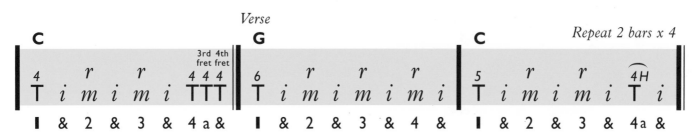

Verse   Repeat 2 bars x 4

C
```
4        r     r              4 4 4
T   i    m  i  m   i          T T T
I   &  2  &  3  &  4 a &
```

G
```
6        r     r     r
T   i    m  i  m   i  m  i
I   &  2  &  3  &  4  &
```

C
```
5        r     r        4H‿
T   i    m  i  m   i     T  i
I   &  2  &  3  &  4 a &
```

I—mag—ine there's   no   hea—ven
it's eas—y   if   you   try
no hell   be—low   us
a-bove us   only   sky.

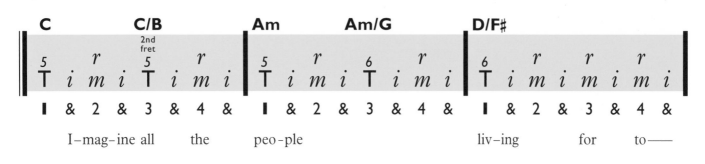

C   **C/B**
```
5       r     5        r
T   i   m  i  T    i    m  i
I   &  2  &  3  &  4  &
```

Am   **Am/G**
```
5       r     6        r
T   i   m  i  T    i    m  i
I   &  2  &  3  &  4  &
```

D/F♯
```
6       r     r        r
T   i   m  i  m   i     m  i
I   &  2  &  3  &  4  &
```

I—mag—ine all   the   peo-ple   liv-ing   for   to——

                              Chorus   Repeat 2 bars x 3

D7
```
↓
I     (2)    (3)    (4)
```

C   **D**
```
5       r   5  4        r
T   i   m  T  T   i     m  i
I   &  2  &  3  &  4  &
```

G   **B7**
```
6       r   5  5        r
T   i   m  T  T   i     m  i
I   &  2  &  3  &  4  &
```

day,   aha.   You may say   I'm a   dreamer
                                              but I'm not the on—ly   one.
                                              I hope some day you'll join us

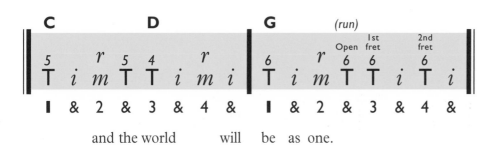

C   **D**
```
5       r   5  4        r
T   i   m  T  T   i     m  i
I   &  2  &  3  &  4  &
```

G   *(run)*
```
6       r   6  6        6
T   i   m  T  T   i     T  i
I   &  2  &  3  &  4  &
```

and the world   will   be as one.

Words & Music by John Lennon

23

Don't Think Twice, It's All Right

Bob Dylan

Alternating Thumb Style

Hammer-ons

In the alternating thumb style a hammer-on often involves a treble string and a pinch:

D

4
P H

I &

The lower curved line means the hammer-on will be on the *treble* string. The 2nd finger is off its usual position in the **D** chord, and hammers down after the pinch. The thumb plays the 4th string and the middle finger the 1st string.

For the hammer-ons in the **Bm**, **A7** and **E7** bars, the 1st finger of the left hand hammers down from the open *2nd string* to the usual fret for the chord.

Bass Runs

Bass runs in alternating thumb patterns are similar to those in the bass-strum style. There are three runs given in the accompaniment. The first from **A7** to **D** (**b c♯ d**), the second from **D7** to **G** (**e f♯ g**), and the last from **G** to **E** (**g f♯ e**).

Use the appropriate fingers for the run notes, and leave the other fingers in position as long as possible.

General

Bob Dylan plays this piece extremely fast. 'Prestissimo' as classical musicians would say, which means over 200 beats per minute! When you've done a lot of practice, put your capo on the 2nd fret and play along with the original recording.

Melody

To make sure you start singing the song in the same key you're playing, here are the notes for the first line:

f♯ f♯   f♯ f♯   f♯ a a   a f♯   d   b
It ain't no use   to sit and wonder why babe

Accompaniment: 4/4 Rhythm

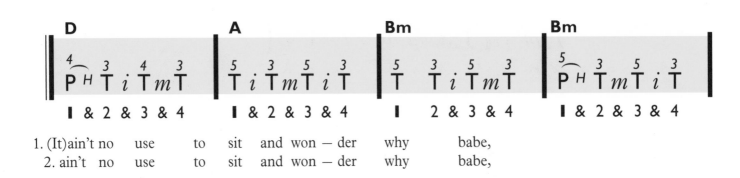

1. (It)ain't no   use   to   sit   and won — der   why   babe,
2. ain't no   use   to   sit   and won — der   why   babe,

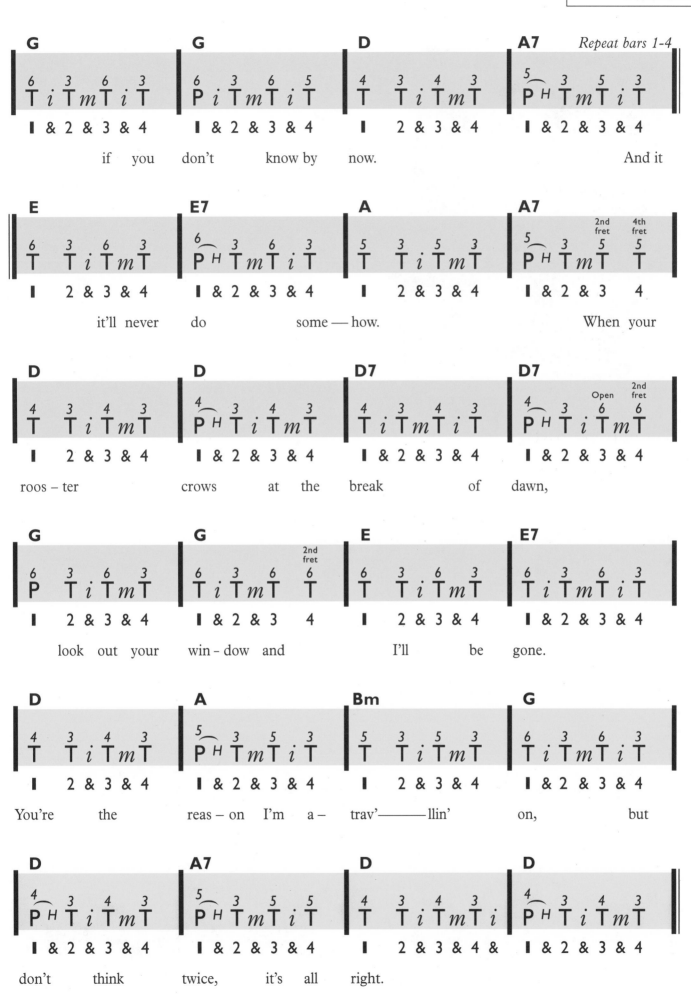

Pinch thumb & middle finger with treble hammer-on

Repeat bars 1-4

if you don't know by now.

And it it'll never do some — how.

When your roos – ter crows at the break of dawn,

look out your win – dow and I'll be gone.

You're the reas – on I'm a – trav'———llin' on, but

don't think twice, it's all right.

Alternating Thumb Style

25

The Boxer

Paul Simon

Use the right hand fingers in the same way as for the arpeggio style. The index finger strikes the 3rd string, the middle strikes the 2nd string, and the ring finger strikes the 1st string. Play the pattern over and over using the correct fingers, then try inventing some variations of your own before having a go at 'The Boxer'.

Three Treble Strings

Using three right hand fingers for alternating patterns gives more variety. Try this pattern:

4/4 Rhythm Hold **G**

⁶		⁴		⁶		⁴	
T	*i*	T	*m*	T	*r*	T	*m*
I	&	2	&	3	&	4	&

Pattern Variations

This arrangement is similar to Paul Simon's original recording, though one or two extra bars of **C** have been omitted. Also, the second verse, not the 1st verse, leads to the chorus. Notice the first bar of **C** where a pinch comes on the 2nd beat and your 3rd finger moves to the 6th string on the 3rd beat. You've already played the run from **C** to **Am** which comes in the 3rd bar.

Check each bar of the accompaniment carefully because there are many slight pattern changes. For variety and more dynamics when playing solo, the bass strum style can be used for the chorus. You then return to alternating thumb patterns for the following verse.

Melody

All the chords and melody notes are in key. Here is the first line:

g g g a g e   e f g g c b a
I am just a poor boy though my story's seldom told

Accompaniment: 4/4 Rhythm

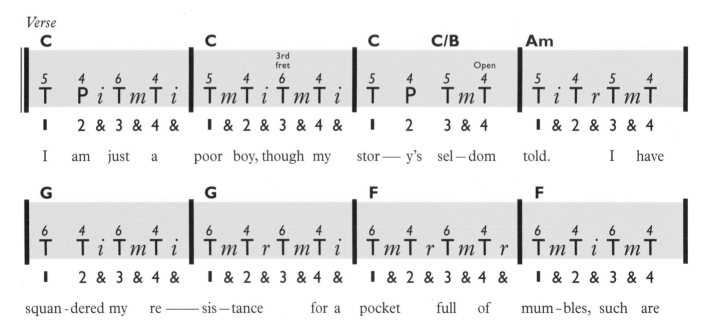

Verse

C | **C** | **C C/B** | **Am**

T P *i* T *m* *i* | T *m* T *i* T *m* T *i* | T P T *m* T | T *i* T *r* T *m* T

I 2 & 3 & 4 & | I & 2 & 3 & 4 & | I 2 3 & 4 | I & 2 & 3 & 4

I am just a poor boy, though my stor — y's sel – dom told. I have

G | **G** | **F** | **F**

T T *i* T *m* T *i* | T *m* T *r* T *m* T *i* | T *m* T *r* T *m* T *r* | T *m* T *i* T *m* T

I 2 & 3 & 4 & | I & 2 & 3 & 4 & | I & 2 & 3 & 4 & | I & 2 & 3 & 4

squan -dered my re ——— sis – tance for a pocket full of mum-bles, such are

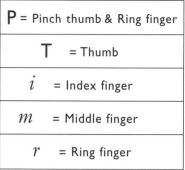

Alternating Thumb Style

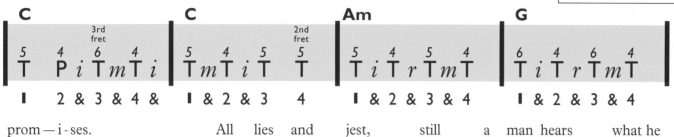

C

3rd fret

| 5 | | 4 | 6 | | 4 |
| T | P | *i* | T | *m* | T | *i* |

| 1 | 2 | & | 3 | & | 4 | & |

prom—i-ses.

C

2nd fret

| 5 | | 4 | 5 | | 5 |
| T | *m* | T | *i* | T | T |

| 1 | & | 2 | & | 3 | 4 |

All   lies   and   jest,   still   a   man hears   what he

Am

| 5 | | 4 | 5 | | 4 |
| T | *i* | T | *r* | T | *m* | T |

| 1 | & | 2 | & | 3 | & | 4 |

G

| 6 | | 4 | 6 | | 4 |
| T | *i* | T | *r* | T | *m* | T |

| 1 | & | 2 | & | 3 | & | 4 |

F

| 6 | | 4 | 6 | | 4 |
| T | *m* | T | *r* | T | *m* | T | *r* |

| 1 | & | 2 | & | 3 | & | 4 | & |

wants   to hear   and

F

| 6 | | 4 | 6 | | 4 |
| T | *m* | T | *i* | T | *m* | T |

| 1 | & | 2 | & | 3 | & | 4 |

dis — re – gards   the   rest.

C

| 5 | | 4 | 5 | | 4 |
| T | *i* | T | *r* | T | *m* | T |

| 1 | & | 2 | & | 3 | & | 4 |

Mm   mm   mm,

G

| 6 | | 4 | 6 | | 4 |
| T | *i* | T | *r* | T | *m* | T |

| 1 | & | 2 | & | 3 | & | 4 |

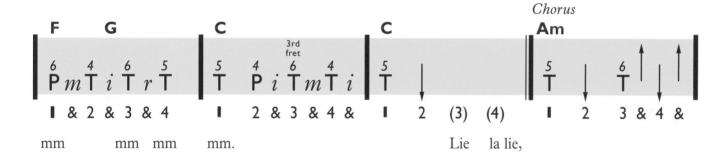

F   **G**

| 6 | | 4 | 6 | | 5 |
| P | *m* | T | *i* | T | *r* | T |

| 1 | & | 2 | & | 3 | & | 4 |

mm   mm mm   mm.

C

3rd fret

| 5 | | 6 | | 4 |
| T | P | *i* | T | *m* | T | *i* |

| 1 | 2 | & | 3 | & | 4 | & |

C

| 5 |
| T   ↓ |

| 1 | 2 | (3) | (4) |

Lie   la lie,

Chorus
Am

| 5 | | 6 | |
| T | ↓ | T | ↑ | ↓ | ↑ |

| 1 | 2 | 3 | & | 4 | & |

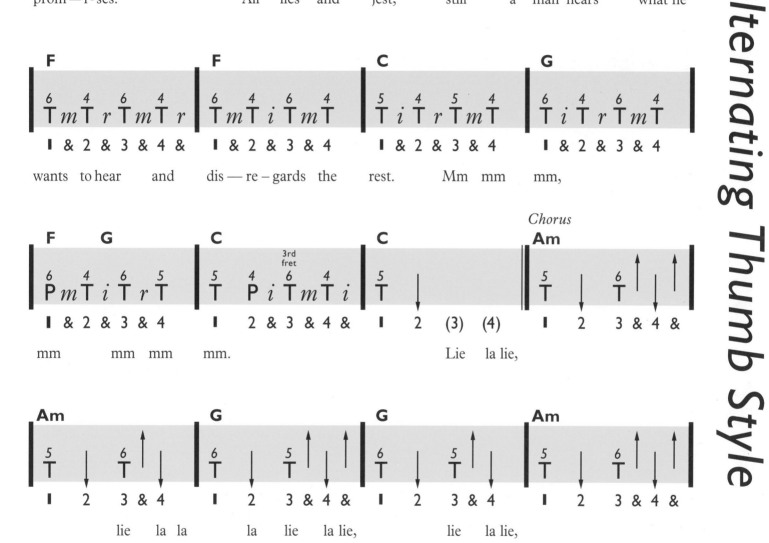

Am

| 5 | | 6 | |
| T | ↓ | T | ↑ | ↓ |

| 1 | 2 | 3 | & | 4 |

lie   la la

G

| 6 | | 5 | |
| T | ↓ | T | ↑ | ↑ |

| 1 | 2 | 3 | & | 4 | & |

la   lie   la lie,

G

| 6 | | 5 | |
| T | ↓ | T | ↑ | ↓ |

| 1 | 2 | 3 | & | 4 |

lie   la lie,

Am

| 5 | | 6 | |
| T | ↓ | T | ↑ | ↓ | ↑ |

| 1 | 2 | 3 | & | 4 | & |

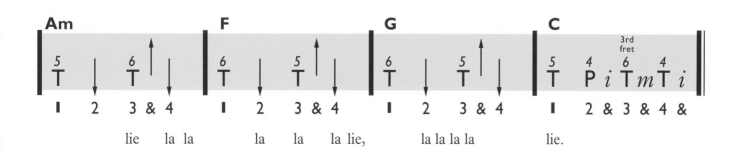

Am

| 5 | | 6 | |
| T | ↓ | T | ↑ | ↓ |

| 1 | 2 | 3 | & | 4 |

lie   la la

F

| 6 | | 5 | |
| T | ↓ | T | ↑ | ↓ |

| 1 | 2 | 3 | & | 4 |

la   la   la lie,

G

| 6 | | 5 | |
| T | ↓ | T | ↑ | ↓ |

| 1 | 2 | 3 | & | 4 |

la la la la

C

3rd fret

| 5 | | 4 | 6 | | 4 |
| T | P | *i* | T | *m* | T | *i* |

| 1 | 2 | & | 3 | & | 4 | & |

lie.

The 59th Street Bridge Song (Feelin' Groovy)

Paul Simon

Alternating Thumb Style

Swing Alternating Thumb

Most swing alternating thumb accompaniments are found in blues and ragtime music, but not all. This Paul Simon song has a swing rhythm, and as before the notes between beats are delayed. Again, in my notation this is shown visually.

G/B Chord

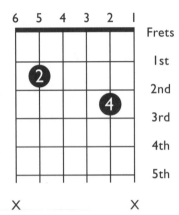

Pattern Variations

Three right hand fingers should be used for this arrangement. When a pinch is indicated, pluck the 1st string with your ring finger except for the **G/B** chord where you strike the 2nd. Notice the syncopation in all the bars except 2 and 5. Move quickly to the **G/B** or **G** chord just before the 3rd beat.

Melody

All the notes and chords are in key for this song. Here is the first line:

e   d   b   c   d   b

Slow down, you move too fast

Accompaniment: 4/4 Swing Rhythm

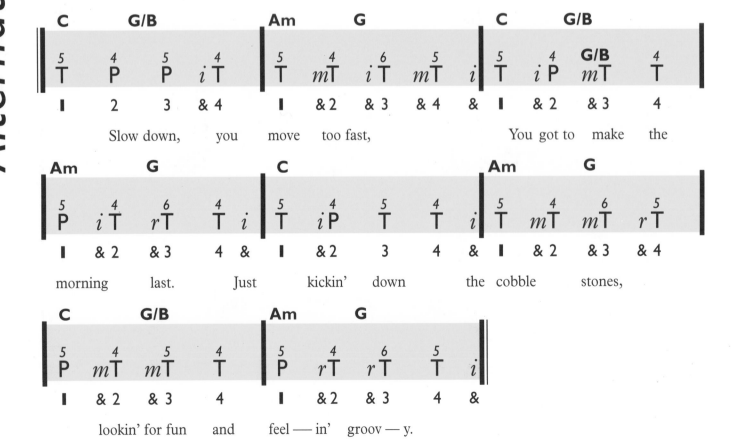

More Ideas

Classical compositions aren't as pattern-like as the modern styles you've been learning. Partly because they stand on their own as instrumentals and need variations from bar to bar and section to section, and partly because they don't involve the normal heavy beat stress of popular music.

So far you've tried just one classical piece, and that was a simple, one-note-at-a-time arrangement. On these next pages there are some intermediate level compositions which explore some more ideas of the classical guitar style.

Follow the information on this page and the notes given before each piece and you shouldn't find them too difficult. Take them very slowly at first.

Rest Signs

As well as signs for note length, there need to be signs for different times of pause, or silence. The note signs were given in Book 2.

Here are the rest signs:

γ = **Quaver rest**

ξ = **Crotchet rest**

▬ = **Minim rest**

▬ = **Semi-breve rest**

Dotted Notes

When notes have a dot placed just after them, they should last half as long again. A minim note with a dot (dotted minim) lasts for the equivalent of three crotchets or 3 beats in 3/4 and 4/4. A dotted crotchet lasts for three quavers or one and a half beats in 3/4 or 4/4.

2/4 Rhythm

Classical music often involves rhythms other than 3/4 and 4/4. When a piece is written in 2/4, the '2' means two beats, and the '4' means each beat is a crotchet in length. So the two stress points are on the first and second crotchets.

Key Signatures

By checking the key signatures at the start of each line of music, you know which notes to play sharp and you can work out the key of the piece. The piece by Carulli ends on a **c** note and has no sharps indicated at the start of each line. This means the key is **C** major.

'Call And Answer' ends with a **G** chord and has one sharp indicated. This means it is written in the key of **G** major. 'Passing Note Waltz' ends on a **d** and has two sharps shown. This means it is written in the key of **D** major.

Try to remember the number of sharps for each key. This will help in understanding and playing all types of music.

Left Hand Fingering

Classical players generally use only the left hand fingers they need at any one time. So in these pieces you can forget about holding whole chord shapes. Work out which fingers are strictly necessary and use only those. Economical use of fingers makes for smoother playing.

Sometimes there may be a choice of finger to use. Experiment with different possibilities and choose the one that you're comfortable with.

Right Hand Fingering

One set of possibilities for right hand fingering is given above the notation for each piece. With notes one after the other on the same string, alternate fingers should normally be used, but again, experiment with different ideas and use the fingering that's best for you.

Applications

Many ideas in classical compositions can be used for arrangements for modern songs. The 'bass-pluck' style used in the Carulli study, for example, can be used successfully in humorous or story-type songs.

Study

Fernando Carulli

Classical Style

Rhythm

This study was written by Fernando Carulli about 170 years ago. Because it's in the 3/4 rhythm, there are three beats per bar and each beat is the equivalent of a crotchet in length.

Key

No sharp (or flat) signs at the start of each line means the piece is in the key of **C** major or **A** minor. Because the last note is **c**, this means the key is **C** major. The last 'chord' is **C**, but try to work out which is the underlying chord for the other bars.

Instrumental: 3/4 Rhythm

Left Hand Fingering

You can use the 1st and 3rd fingers in the 4th bar, or the 2nd and 4th. In the 7th bar the 2nd finger can be used for the low **g** note, with the 1st playing the **a** note that follows. Or you could use the 3rd and 2nd fingers.

Passing Note Waltz

Russ Shipton

| T = Thumb |
| *i* = Index finger |
| *m* = Middle finger |
| *r* = Ring finger |

Two Part Notation

The last piece was written as one part, but really the music involves two distinct parts: the treble (melody) and the bass (rhythm and harmony).

In this piece I've separated bass and treble parts by using note stems that go down and up respectively. You'll see that each part must add up to three crotchets of time (three beats here) for each bar. Work out the timing of each part, then put them together.

Instrumental: 3/4 Rhythm
Standard Musical Notation

Classical Style

Key

What major scale has two sharp notes? Check the last note as well and you'll work out the key very quickly. Try to discover the underlying chords for each bar.

If you played the piece using full chord shapes, try playing it again using only the fingers actually needed.

Passing Notes

The treble passing notes (run notes) are easy to find. Raise a finger that's down or add another. In the 3rd and 6th bars, for example, you can add your 3rd finger for the **d** note on the 2nd string.

Call And Answer

Russ Shipton

General

As the title suggests, this piece involves a switch from a treble to a bass line, and back again - a sort of question and answer arrangement that is used sometimes in Indian music, pop and blues, and also in opera. In the first bar let the bass ring on for the whole duration (two beats), while in the second bar make sure the treble note rings for the full bar.

Key

The sharp sign at the start of each line of notation means you're in the key of **G** major. There are two 'accidentals' (called such because they are not in the major scale of **G**) in the 6th and 7th bars, so they have a sharp sign before them. The other sign, in the 2nd, 4th, 10th and 12th bars, is called a 'natural' and simply means that you ignore the key signature wherever you see one.

Instrumental: 2/4 Rhythm

Classical Style

(Strum)

Jamaica Farewell

Verse 1
Down the way where the nights are gay
And the sun shines daily on the mountain top
I took a trip on a sailing ship
And when I reached Jamaica I made a stop.

Chorus
But I'm sad to say that I'm on my way
Won't be back for many a day
My heart is down, my head is turning around
I had to leave a little girl in Kingston Town.

Verse 2
Down in the market you can hear
Ladies cry out as on their heads they bear
"Akai rice, salt fish are nice"
And the rum is fine any time of year.

Verse 3
Sounds of laughter everywhere
And the dancing girls swing to and fro'
I must declare my heart is there
Though I've been from Maine to Mexico.

Lyrics

Wonderwall

Verse 1

Today is gonna be the day that they're gonna throw
    it back to you
By now you should have somehow realised what
    you gotta do
I don't believe that anybody feels the way I do about
    you now.

Verse 2

Back beat, the word is on the street that the fire in
    your heart is out
I'm sure you've heard it all before, but you never
    really had a doubt
I don't believe that anybody feels the way I do
    Em7 G Dsus4 A7sus4
about you now.

Bridge 1

And all the roads we have to walk are winding
And all the lights that lead us there are blinding
There are many things that I would like to say to
    you but I don't know how.

Chorus

Because maybe, you're gonna be the one that saves me
And after all, you're my wonderwall.

Verse 3

Today was gonna be the day but they'll never
    throw it back to you
By now you should've somehow realised what you're
    not to do
I don't believe that anybody feels the way I do
    about you now.

Bridge 2

And all the roads that lead you there were winding
And all the lights that light the way are blinding
There are many things that I would like to say to you
But I don't know how.

Don't Look Back In Anger

Verse 1

Slip inside the eye of your mind
Don't you know you might find a better place to play
You said that you'd never been
But all the things that you've seen slowly fade away

Bridge 1

So I start a revolution from my bed
'Cause you said the brains I had went to my head
Step outside, Summertime's in bloom
Stand up beside the fireplace
Take that look from off your face
You ain't ever gonna burn my heart out.

Chorus

And so Sally can wait, she knows it's too late
As we're walking on by
Her soul slides away, "But don't look back in anger"
I heard you say.

Verse 2

Take me to the place where you go
Where nobody knows if it's night or day
But please don't put your life in the hands
Of a rock 'n' roll band who'll throw it all away.

Bridge 2

I'm gonna start a revolution from my bed
'Cause you said the brains I had went to my head
Step outside, 'cause Summertime's in bloom
Stand up beside the fireplace
Take that look from off your face
'Cause you ain't ever gonna burn my heart out.

Chorus 2

And so Sally can wait, she knows it's too late
As she's walking on by
My soul slides away, 'But don't look back in anger'
I heard you say.

34

Lay Down Sally

Verse 1

There is nothing that is wrong in wanting you to
    stay here with me
I know you've got somewhere to go, but won't you
    make yourself at home and stay with me?
And don't you ever leave.

Chorus

Lay down Sally, and rest here in my arms
Don't you think you want someone to talk to?
Lay down Sally, no need to leave so soon
I've been trying all night long just to talk to you.

Verse 2

The sun ain't nearly on the rise and we still got
    the moon and stars above
Underneath the velvet skies, love is all that matters
    won't you stay with me?
And don't you ever leave.

Verse 3

I long to see the morning light, colouring your
    face so dreamily
So don't you go and say goodbye, you can lay your
    worries down and stay with me
And don't you ever leave.

Can't Buy Me Love

Intro

Bm Em Bm Em
Can't buy me lo—ve, lo—ve
Am D7
Can't buy me lo—ve.

Verse 1

I'll buy you a diamond ring, my friend
If it makes you feel all right
I'll get you anything, my friend
If it makes you feel all right
'Cause I don't care too much for money
Money can't buy me love.

Verse 2

I'll give you all I've got to give
If you say you love me too
I may not have a lot to give
But what I've got I'll give to you
I don't care too much for money
Money can't buy me love.

Chorus

Can't buy me love, everybody tells me so
Can't buy me love, no no no, no.

Verse 3

Say you don't need no diamond rings
And I'll be satisfied
Tell me that you want the kind of things
That money just can't buy
I don't care too much for money
Money can't buy me love.

Bm Em Bm Em
Can't buy me lo—ve, lo—ve
Am D7 G7
Can't buy me lo—ve.

Lyrics

She'll Be Coming Round The Mountain

Verse 1
She'll be coming round the mountain when
    she comes (x2)
She'll be coming round the mountain (x2)
She'll be coming round the mountain when she comes.

Verse 2
She'll be driving six white horses when she comes (x2)
She'll be driving six white horses (x2)
She'll be driving six white horses when she comes.

Verse 3
She'll be wearing pink pyjamas when she comes (x2)
She'll be wearing pink pyjamas (x2)
She'll be wearing pink pyjamas when she comes.

Verse 4
She will have to sleep with Grandma when
    she comes (x2)
She will have to sleep with Grandma (x2)
She will have to sleep with Grandma when she comes.

Verse 5
And we'll all go to meet her when she comes (x2)
And we'll all go to meet her (x2)
Oh we'll all go to meet her when she comes.

Suzanne

Verse 1
Suzanne takes you down to her place near the river
You can hear the boats go by, you can spend the
    night beside her
And you know that she's half crazy, but that's why
    you want to be there
And she feeds you tea and oranges that come all the
    way from China
And just when you mean to tell her that you have no
    love to give her
She gets you on her wavelength and she lets the
    river answer
That you've always been her lover.

Chorus
And you want to travel with her
And you want to travel blind
And you know that she will trust you
For you've touched her perfect body with your mind.

Verse 2
And Jesus was a sailor when he walked upon the water
And he spent a long time watching from his lonely
    wooden tower
And when he knew for certain only drowning men
    could see him
He said "All men will be sailors then until the sea
    shall free them"
But he himself was broken long before the sky
    would open
Foresaken, almost human, he sank beneath your
    wisdom like a stone.

Chorus 2
And you want to travel with him
And you want to travel blind
And you think maybe you'll trust him
For he's touched your perfect body with his mind.

Verse 3
Now Suzanne takes your hand and she leads you to
    the river
She is wearing rags and feathers from Salvation
    Army counters
And the sun pours down like honey on our lady of
    the harbour
And she shows you where to look among the garbage
    and the flowers
There are heroes in the seaweed, there are children in
    the morning
They are leaning out for love, and they will lean that
    way forever
While Suzanne holds the mirror.

Chorus 3
And you want to travel with her
And you want to travel blind
And you know that you can trust her
For she's touched your perfect body with her mind.

Always On My Mind

Verse 1
Maybe I didn't treat you
Quite as good as I should have
Maybe I didn't love you
Quite as often as I could have
Little things I should have said and done
I just never took the time
You were always on my mind
You were always on my mind.

Verse 2
Maybe I didn't hold you
All those lonely, lonely times
And I guess I never told you
I'm so happy that you're mine
If I made you feel second best
Girl I'm so sorry I was blind
You were always on my mind
You were always on my mind.

Middle Section
 C Am F   **Dm**
Tell me, tell me that your sweet love hasn't died
 C Am   **F**
Give me give me one more chance
                   G   **C**
    to keep you satisfied satisfied.

Imagine

Verse 1
Imagine there's no heaven
It's easy if you try
No hell below us
Above us only sky
Imagine all the people living for today, aha..

Verse 2
Imagine there's no countries
It isn't hard to do
Nothing to kill or die for
And no religion too
Imagine all the people living life in peace, aha..

Chorus
You may say I'm a dreamer
But I'm not the only one
I hope some day you'll join us
And the world will be as one.

Verse 3
Imagine no possessions
I wonder if you can
No need for greed or hunger
A brotherhood of man
Imagine all the people, sharing all the world, aha..

Don't Think Twice, It's All Right

Verse 1

It ain't no use to sit and wonder why babe
If you don't know by now
And it ain't no use to sit and wonder why, babe
It'll never do somehow
When your rooster crows at the break of dawn
Look out your window and I'll be gone
You're the reason I'm a-travellin' on
But don't think twice, it's all right.

Verse 2

It ain't no use in turnin' on your light babe
The light I never knowed
And it ain't no use in turnin' on your light babe
I'm on the dark side of the road
But I wish there was something you would do or say
To try and make me change my mind and stay
But we never did too much talkin' anyway
But don't think twice, it's all right.

Verse 3

So it ain't no use in callin' out my name gal
Like you never done before
And it ain't no use in callin' out my name gal
I can't hear you anymore
I'm a-thinkin' and a-wonderin' walkin' down the road
I once loved a woman, a child I'm told
I give her my heart but she wanted my soul
But don't think twice, it's all right.

Verse 4

So long honey babe
Where I'm bound, I can't tell
But goodbye's too good a word babe
So I'll just say "Fare thee well"
I ain't a-sayin' you treated me unkind
You could have done better but I don't mind
You just kinda wasted my precious time
But don't think twice, it's all right.

The Boxer

Verse 1

I am just a poor boy, though my story's seldom told
I have squandered my resistance for a pocketful of
    mumbles, such are promises
All lies and jest, still a man hears what he wants to hear
    and disregards the rest.

Verse 2

When I left my home and my family, I was no more
    than a boy
In the company of strangers, in the quiet of a railway
    station, running scared
Laying low, seeking out the poorer quarters where the
    ragged people go
Looking for the places only they would know.

Chorus

Lie la lie, lie la la la la lie la lie
Lie la lie, lie la la la la la la lie la la la la lie.

Verse 3

Asking only workman's wages, I come looking for a job
But I get no offers, just a come-on from the whores on
    Seventh Avenue
I do declare there were times when I was so lonesome,
    I took some comfort there
Ooh la la, la la la la.

Verse 4

Then I'm laying out my winter clothes and wishing
    I was gone
Going home, where the New York City winters aren't
    C   **C C**
bleeding me,
         Em Am   **G G C C**
Leading me,   going home.

Verse 5

In the clearing stands a boxer and a fighter by his trade
And he carries the reminders of every glove that laid
    him down
Or cut him till he cried out in his anger and his shame
"I am leaving, I am leaving" but the fighter still
    remains.

**The 59th Street Bridge Song
(Feelin' Groovy)**

Verse 1
Slow down, you move too fast
You've got to make the morning last
Just kicking down the cobble stones
Lookin' for fun and feelin' groovy.

Verse 2
Hello lamppost, watcha knowin'?
I've come to watch your flowers growin'
Ain'tcha got no rhymes for me?
Dootin' doo-doo, feelin' groovy.

Verse 3
I got no deeds to do, no promises to keep
I'm dappled and drowsy and ready to sleep
Let the morning time drop all its petals on me
Life, I love you, all is groovy.

Closing Comments

Congratulations!

You've worked successfully through all three of *The Complete Guitar Player* course books and are now a competent and versatile guitarist. You've mastered patterns and techniques in four distinct and popular right hand styles which you can use to play a wide variety of rock, pop, folk and country songs. You've also had a useful introduction to the classical style and music theory.

But don't stop here, of course. There's a wealth of material out there that you can start playing right now. To progress further with your guitar playing, why not check out the supplementary books in the *The Complete Guitar Player* series, including the Tablature Book, and a huge range of songbooks including many popular songs.

See the complete Music Sales catalogue for full details of these and many other great guitar books (details right).

I hope that you have enjoyed this course and will continue to learn and play the guitar.

Good luck!

Exclusive distributors:
Music Sales Limited
8/9 Frith Street, London W1D 3JB, England.
Music Sales Pty Limited
120 Rothschild Avenue, Rosebery, NSW 2018, Australia.

Order No. AM953183 (Book & CD edition).
Order No. AM964183 (Book only).
This book © Copyright 2000 by Wise Publications.

Written and arranged by Russ Shipton.
Edited by Sorcha Armstrong.
Cover and book design by Michael Bell Design.
Cover and guitar photography by George Taylor.
Guitars supplied by Rhodes Music.
Artist photographs courtesy of
    London Features International and Retna.
Music processed by Paul Ewers Music Design.
Printed in the United Kingdom by
    Caligraving Limited, Thetford, Norfolk.

CD programmed by John Moores.
All guitars by Arthur Dick.
Engineered by Kester Sims.

Your guarantee of quality:
As publishers, we strive to produce every book
to the highest commercial standards.
The music has been freshly engraved and the book
has carefully designed to minimise awkward page turns
and to make playing from it a real pleasure.
Particular care has been given to specifying
acid-free, neutral-sized paper made from pulps
which have not been elemental chlorine bleached.
This pulp is from farmed sustainable forests and
was produced with special regard for the environment.
Throughout, the printing and binding have been
planned to ensure a sturdy, attractive publication
which should give years of enjoyment.
If your copy fails to meet our high standards, please
inform us and we will gladly replace it.

Music Sales' complete catalogue describes
thousands of titles and is available in full colour
sections by subject, direct from Music Sales Limited.
Please state your areas of interest and send a
cheque/postal order for £1.50 for postage to:
Music Sales Limited, Newmarket Road, Bury St. Edmunds,
Suffolk IP33 3YB.

www.musicsales.com

2/01 (39525)